Want More? ...

Why You Should Expect Double Digit Returns When You Invest !

By

K. Allan Henderson

September 2, 2014

Want More? ...

Why You Should Expect Double Digit Returns When You Invest !

When I decided to embark on this adventure, and it is an adventure, I wanted to come up with a way to make real money. I mean, don't we all? Well, it's the capitalistic way. Then, I thought, I really need to come up with a way to offer something of value to whoever would eventually read this. At the same time, I wanted to be as brief and to the point as possible, but again, still offering something of substance. In addition, it had to be memorable.

The following pages will be brief, but I would like to think that you will find the information helpful and something that you would be willing to recommend to a friend, whether by word of mouth, face to face or via the digital information wave.

So part of the title of this book is do you "Want More?" The other part of the title is "Why Should You Expect Double Digit Returns?" I know I want more, whether it's in just life in general or more specifically, in wealth. Then again, wealth can mean many things to many people. One can have a wealth of knowledge, a wealth of close friends, or let's face it, a wealth of money.

I'd like to focus on the wealth of money. I will tell you right off the bat that I am what I call a wealth of money in training type of guy. My goal here is really to take you as the reader along with me on my journey to become wealthy. I'm gaining the wealth of knowledge and I'm just within reach of gaining my wealth of riches. The thing of it is though, I think that in order to get where I'd like to be in the money game, I know that I need to offer something of value to the public.

So here is my offering to you. Take the time to read through these next few pages and really get what I'm saying because there is an opportunity here for you to expand your knowledge and thus expand your opportunity to increase your wealth.

I want more. Do you want more? Of course you do. Ok, here it is...

Find a quiet area and sit down. Ask yourself what you want to accomplish in life, really want to accomplish. Then ask yourself how does that which you want to do offers value to society. Once you figure out what you have a passion for and how that result can be turned into a way to offer value to society, you have half the battle won. For example, say you have a passion for taking pictures. How can you take pictures in a way that those pictures become something of value to others aside from yourself? The next step is how do you "monetize" those pictures of value to the public for yourself in a way of making it a win win situation. When I say win win situation, I mean that both you and those who take you up on your offer benefit from the offering.

Part of me writing this brief book is that I feel that I have a message to share and I believe that it is of value to someone. I feel that this value is real and that others will see it as such also. I'm not claiming to be some guru or master of knowledge, but more of a vessel that is being used to "open" the eyes of those willing to learn just a little for their overall growth.

By now, you should definitely be asking yourself, do I want more and have I gained just a little bit more knowledge up to this point? Maybe you have, or maybe you haven't. I hope you have.

Now in order to create and/or grow your money wealth, there are many, many ways to do so, but you have to be open to diverse ideas. There can be wealth gained by investing in the stock market, pursuing a new business venture, investing in real estate, etc. I like the idea of investing in real estate as well as other entrepreneurial opportunities. Of course, before I would invest in something like real estate, I would pursue as much information as possible before making the decision to invest. Just by doing a little searching on the internet on real estate investing, there is a "wealth" of information out there. Whether it's sourced from attending investment clubs, reading articles, reading books, attending phone conferences, attending webinars, or even attending a "Live" real estate seminar, there's so much information out there.

Think of the photography example. You could do a search on photography and there would be a vast amount of information out there on the internet. Before you'd go make a decision to spend any of your hard earned money on investing in more information on photography to fulfill a dream of yours, you'd want to get as much good information as possible about it.

That's what I'd suggest about any type of money investment you are thinking of making. Personally, I've attended numerous conference calls, webinars, and seminars, as well as read many books and training manuals, listened to CD's, and viewed DVD and on-line video content on many different types of entrepreneurial ventures. My favorite though has always been the information I've gained on investing in real estate. I've even had the opportunity to invest in a little myself. I've had the opportunity to buy, fix up, and rent, as well as buy, fix up, and sell for a profit and passive income.

I've always been amazed at the way so many people are able to realize their dream of financial independence or more correctly, financial freedom when they follow their dream and make it a reality. Real estate is a one of the quickest ways of realizing financial freedom. For those of you not familiar with the term, financial freedom is achieved when your income (importantly, passive income) exceeds your expenses (the money you're paying out) and you start to be able to enjoy life without the stress of worrying about how or when a bill is going to be paid. As I mentioned, I'm working towards that goal myself.

I'm the wiser now and a step closer towards that dream of financial freedom.

Another entrepreneurial area that is really peaking my interest these days is in the area of internet marketing. There are so many different ways to generate real income just by using your laptop and connecting with the right resources. The social networking monetizing opportunities on such popular platforms as facebook, twitter, etc. are almost mindboggling.

The revenues you can earn from running ads on your various websites or earning commissions from selling various products on line are almost endless. I've had a taste of it and now I'm focusing a lot of my efforts here as well. There are numerous books about how to do this, but one of my favorites is the "The LapTop Millionaire" by Mark Anastasi.

You really have to pick a strategy, a niche, and a passion and just create a plan from a proven formula and commit to the execution of the plan. Another couple of great resources are "Rich Dad, Poor Dad" and "Think and Grow Rich." If you want to learn how to create wealth, how to be financially free, and how to "KEEP" it, then these are books that will get your mind thinking in the right direction.

Now shifting gears a little, in order to get those double digit returns on investment, I'd like to focus on one of the best ways I've been educated on how to do so and that's in the area of real estate. You may have heard that it is the quickest way to gain wealth and financial freedom. There are many, many ways you can invest in real estate. You can be the person buying the real estate yourself, or you could be the person providing the funds for another investor to buy the investment themselves.

Also, as with so many successful businesses, building relationships is instrumental for the business to grow and thrive. I've met so many people in my journey towards entrepreneurial success. I currently run a successful business with my wife in the healthcare field (see us at www.tranquilityassistedlivinghome.com) helping the senior population. We utilized our knowledge and experience in real estate to help maintain the property we have to run this business. I also take the lead in running real estate business (check out one of our sites at www.dignolonanneeded.com) that we have which currently is primarily focusing on property management. However, I plan on branching into other, more active investing areas in 2014. As I mentioned, we've bought, fixed up, sold, and rented property, but not on the scale that I'd like to be at. I also maintain a blog (www.goodsmallbusinessideas.net) that contains a wealth of information on business opportunities for small business owners. Take a look as there might be something out there on the site that could be beneficial to you. Part of the reason for me writing this brief book is to put some of my thoughts in writing to share with others to let them know that their dreams are possible.

Whether it's writing a book, getting into internet marketing, investing in real estate, or whatever you can dream up, my message is to follow those dreams and NEVER let anyone be a naysayer and keep you from pursuing your dreams. As the saying goes, "if you can dream it, you can achieve it."

Now back to those double digit returns. If you're less than impressed with the returns you may be earning on your savings, whether regular savings or retirement savings, something you may want to consider would be to be a private money lender to a real estate investor. Say you have a CD (3 yr or less) or a regular savings account earning you less than 1.5% or in most cases less than 1% and you want more. Now if you were invested in the bond market or stock market, depending on what you were invested in and when you invested, you could have made a descent return.   The S&P 500 had a recent yearly return of almost 18% on average, and almost 11.3% over the last 3 years on average. The US bond market on average over the last year has had a return of about 4.5%. It really depends on the amount of risk you're willing to take for the return that you desire.

Now, depending on the terms of the agreement with your real estate investor, you can earn rates from say 8% up to 15% or more just by lending your money. You may lend it for 3 months or 6 months depending on the agreement and real estate deal on the table. Now if you're taking on more of a roll other than just lending money, say bringing some expertise such as construction, you may agree to enter into some sort of short term partnership and potentially earn up to 50%. It really depends upon what you and the real estate investor are looking to accomplish as you enter into an agreement.

One of the types of deals that I'm looking to pursue in 2014 is to find individuals who are looking to invest a portion of their investible savings for a short term period, say three to six months, for a 12% to 15% return on earnings or profits. The nice thing about these type of returns compared to a 12% to 15% return in the stock market is that you can potentially invest your money 2 to 4 times in real estate in one year for up to 24% to 60% total overall return. Of course, no returns are guaranteed, but with your investment secured by the real estate property you're investing in, you can tend to have a lower risk for the return compared to the risk return reward investing in the stock market.

If this type of opportunity sounds like something you might be interested in, take a look at this website (www.diginvestmentgroupbargainhouses.com) for information on what we do and enter some info so that we may contact you.

Now, as I mentioned from the beginning, this book is a brief one, but one I thought I had to share. I hope that after reading this you decide to really sit back and think about what you want in life financially. Are you satisfied with where you are? Are you ok just getting by? Do you want to be financially free? Do you want massive passive income? Do you want wealth of great proportions? Do you Want More? Should you expect double digit returns when you invest? If you are looking to make a positive financial change in your life, you must educate yourself and take action. I've had numerous mentors on my way towards success and I continue to look for others that I can learn more from.

Always keep an open mind and be willing to increase you knowledge. As one of my mentors has said, you can make money and lose it, but if you have the knowledge, that can't be taken away from you. You can use that knowledge and experience to make that money and more back. It's an old saying that goes something like this: give a man a fish and he'll have for food a day, but teach a man to fish and he'll never go hungry. That's just like with knowledge. Someone can give you money and you'll have it to spend until it is gone, but if you have the financial knowledge of wealth creation and how to properly grow it, a minor "hiccup" won't keep you down. You'll know how to make even more money and probably in a faster period of time with even bigger financial results.

As I begin to close, my last thoughts for you are to never let the naysayers talk you out of pursuing your financial dreams. Remember the definition of insanity is "doing the same thing over and over and expecting a different result." If you want financial success, you have to be willing to do something different from what you're doing now, get educated, research thoroughly, and TAKE ACTION.

Good luck in your journey and I hope to hear from you. I wish you massive SUCCESS!

Definition of **Insanity**....

Doing the same ...

... thing over and over...

... again, and ...

... expecting a ...

... different result.

The only way....

... that you will have truly ...

... a successful path ...

... towards financial freedom...

YOU MUST TAKE ACTION !!!

In order to have MASSIVE SUCCESS...

... YOU MUST REMEMBER THE DEFINITION OF INSANITY ...

...AND not allow yourself to be saddled by the naysayers, AND ...

...REMEMBER your deep down WHY for wanting to be successful, AND...

...TAKE the plunge to Take Action to have MASSIVE SUCCESS!!! Creating and pursuing opportunities for PASSIVE INCOME is one of the best ways to ensure continued Financial Freedom. If you can generate income while you're on vacation, playing (and yes, we all have to play and have fun ☺), and just doing anything other than working, you are going in the right direction. Having your business on autopilot and making you money even when you're away is the ultimate goal. Of course, you will have to spend time on getting the business up and running on the front end to create that passive income for you on the back end, but after you've put the "time in" initially, you'll be saying it was all worth it. There will be some continual small increments of time given to the business ongoing, but nothing like when you were initially forming it. Just remember, " Passive Income leads to Financial Freedom."

Also, remember to Take Action, because if you want to change your life, you have to always tell yourself not to forget the definition of "insanity" as you want to be willing to "change" in order to bring Financial Success to your Life sooner rather than later.

I wish Much Success to You!!!

...and as many of my mentors currently say, "I'll see YOU on the Other Side!"